T0370493

52
WEEKS
OF
M.I.R.A.C.L.E.S.

RAE LASHEA

iUniverse books may be ordered through booksellers or by contacting:

iUniverse
1663 Liberty Drive
Bloomington, IN 47403
www.iuniverse.com
1-800-Authors (1-800-288-4677)

Because of the dynamic nature of the Internet, any web addresses or links contained in this book may have changed since publication and may no longer be valid. The views expressed in this work are solely those of the author and do not necessarily reflect the views of the publisher, and the publisher hereby disclaims any responsibility for them.

Any people depicted in stock imagery provided by Getty Images are models,
and such images are being used for illustrative purposes only.
Certain stock imagery © Getty Images.

ISBN: 978-1-5320-9961-8 (sc)
ISBN: 978-1-5320-9962-5 (e)

Library of Congress Control Number: 2020907771

Print information available on the last page.

iUniverse rev. date: 04/29/2020

Fifty-Two Weeks

of

M.I.R.A.C.L.E.S

Rae Lashea

This literary gem is dedicated to:

My Nieces: Tanisha, Elena, Asha, Sierra, Lyric

&

My Nephews: Armando, Howie, Armand, Andy, Lee, Arval, Sankofa, Andre, Amare

May MIRACLES happen each day for you, to you, and because of you!

Introduction:

Fifty-Two Weeks of M.I.R.A.C.L.E.S. is about appreciating all that is wonderful and good on this planet. Through prayer, meditation, visioning or whatever practice we use to convene and converse with God, Spirit, Source, whatever divine I AM we believe in, we become closer to that from which we originate and are awakened to the secrets of the Universe.

Regular and consistent practice is key to understanding ourselves, life, and our place within this realm of existence. With all of our activities, demands, and life's little quirks that tug and pull on us daily, it can be difficult carving out that time and space to connect with The One in order to "let the Spirit renew your thoughts and attitudes". The goal is to do the practice until the practice does you; where there is a yearning, a pulling, a craving to communicate with Divinity as habitual as it is to brush your teeth, take a shower, drink a glass of water. Understanding the benefit and advantage of taking just a few minutes each day, of course this can and will grow over time, to immerse ourselves in the art of remembering to remember that there is a higher being that allows love, peace, joy, and beauty to exist around us, is crucial to putting in the time and doing the work. After all, we are worth it.

"*Fifty Two Weeks*" is designed to outline and highlight M.I.R.A.C.L.E.S. that exist and take place through, in, as and around us. Each "MIRACLE" is an acronym and is intended to be the focused phrase of contemplation, meditation, consideration, and reflection for an entire week. Whether we are sitting quietly, driving, jogging, washing dishes, folding clothes, in line at the grocery store or bank, in the waiting room at the doctor's office, or walking our dog, we can remember to remember that we are instrumental in a dynamic and unfolding world and each commune with the unseen brings us closer to understanding the mysteries of the invisible, tapping into Source, and unlocking and utilizing the power of the cosmos right at your fingertips.

Start today! Write out the acronym and put it in the place or places you'll visit often: your bathroom mirror, your car visor or dashboard, your computer, office desk, or agenda book. If you're up for the challenge, memorize it. Wherever and whatever it is that will remind you to notice it, utter it out loud, and reflect on the phrase, is what you should do. Say it daily, multiple times if you can. All of these MIRACLES are inspired, not duplicating a word in any phrase. Think about them; ponder their meaning and the greater meaning behind each of them daily for a week at a time. In one year, that is fifty two weeks, you will have opened your heart, mind, and all six senses to a greater love, joy, peace, fullness, beauty, understanding and appreciation of yourself, your life, your world, and everyone and thing in it and that's just the beginning. Whatever your purpose on this planet is will unveil itself to you along with the steps needed to achieve it. If you'll dare to do the work, listen, and obey, your life, along with all the infinite possibilities will unfold before your very eyes.

Today's Date: _____

1.

Moving
Insurmountable
Roadblocks
Acquiring
Clarity and
Lasting
Explanations of
Science

Notes & Reflections (i.e. *how can I apply this in my life? What words or phrases resonate with me? What MIRACLE or part of the miracle do I feel connected to? Disconnected from?*):

_____
_____
_____
_____
_____
_____
_____
_____
_____

2.
Matching
Inspiration and
Realism
Achieving
Controls
Locating and
Eliminating
Stress

Notes & Reflections (i.e. *how can I apply this in my life? What words or phrases resonate with me? What MIRACLE or part of the miracle do I feel connected to? Disconnected from?*):

_____

_____

_____

_____

_____

_____

_____

_____

3.

Mastering
Ingenuity
Removing
Agitating
Conditions
Leaving
Emptiness
Stagnant

Notes & Reflections (i.e. *how can I apply this in my life? What words or phrases resonate with me? What MIRACLE or part of the miracle do I feel connected to? Disconnected from?*):

_____

_____

_____

_____

_____

_____

_____

_____

_____

4.

Moments
Indescribably
Revealing
Art
Culture
Language and
Extraordinary
Style

Notes & Reflections (i.e. *how can I apply this in my life? What words or phrases resonate with me? What MIRACLE or part of the miracle do I feel connected to? Disconnected from?*):

_____

_____

_____

_____

_____

_____

_____

_____

5.

Manifesting
Intelligent
Reasonable
Absolute
Conclusions
Liberating
Ecstasy and
Splendor

Notes & Reflections (i.e. *how can I apply this in my life? What words or phrases resonate with me? What MIRACLE or part of the miracle do I feel connected to? Disconnected from?*):

_____

_____

_____

_____

_____

_____

_____

_____

_____

6.
Making
It
Real
Although
Contaminating
Lies
Emerge
Seductively

Notes & Reflections (i.e. *how can I apply this in my life? What words or phrases resonate with me? What MIRACLE or part of the miracle do I feel connected to? Disconnected from?*):

_____

_____

_____

_____

_____

_____

_____

_____

_____

7.
Majestic
Intervention
Regarding
Affairs and
Choices
Limiting
Errors and
Setbacks

Notes & Reflections (i.e. *how can I apply this in my life? What words or phrases resonate with me? What MIRACLE or part of the miracle do I feel connected to? Disconnected from?*):

_____

_____

_____

_____

_____

_____

_____

_____

_____

8.

Mountainous
Impossibilities
Rendered
Attainable through
Conscious
Listening
Exploration and
Sacrifice

Notes & Reflections (i.e. *how can I apply this in my life? What words or phrases resonate with me? What MIRACLE or part of the miracle do I feel connected to? Disconnected from?*):

_____

_____

_____

_____

_____

_____

_____

_____

_____

_____

9.

Marvelous

Inception

Reaching

All time

Climactic

Levels

Experienced through

Silence

Notes & Reflections (i.e. *how can I apply this in my life? What words or phrases resonate with me? What MIRACLE or part of the miracle do I feel connected to? Disconnected from?*):

_____

_____

_____

_____

_____

_____

_____

_____

_____

10.

Marriages

Illuminated in

Radiant

Amour

Cosmic

Love

Exemplifying

Soul mates

Notes & Reflections (i.e. *how can I apply this in my life? What words or phrases resonate with me? What MIRACLE or part of the miracle do I feel connected to? Disconnected from?*):

_____

_____

_____

_____

_____

_____

_____

_____

_____

11.
Maternal
Instinct
Rearing
All
Children
Lovingly and
Educating
Sternly

Notes & Reflections (i.e. *how can I apply this in my life? What words or phrases resonate with me? What MIRACLE or part of the miracle do I feel connected to? Disconnected from?*):

_____

_____

_____

_____

_____

_____

_____

_____

_____

12.
Microscopic
Inclinations
Reaffirming
Awesome
Capabilities
Lying
Erroneously
Subdued

Notes & Reflections (i.e. *how can I apply this in my life? What words or phrases resonate with me? What MIRACLE or part of the miracle do I feel connected to? Disconnected from?*):

_____

_____

_____

_____

_____

_____

_____

_____

_____

_____

13.

Motion
Idle
Ruminating
Assembled
Carefully
Liberated
Executed
Strongly

Notes & Reflections (i.e. *how can I apply this in my life? What words or phrases resonate with me? What MIRACLE or part of the miracle do I feel connected to? Disconnected from?*):

_____

_____

_____

_____

_____

_____

_____

_____

_____

14.
Melodic
Instruction
Revealed
After
Careful
Lulling of
External
Static

Notes & Reflections (i.e. *how can I apply this in my life? What words or phrases resonate with me? What MIRACLE or part of the miracle do I feel connected to? Disconnected from?*):

_____

_____

_____

_____

_____

_____

_____

_____

_____

15.
Many
Instances of
Realization
Acknowledging
Conscious
Levels of
Evolution
Sincerely

Notes & Reflections (i.e. *how can I apply this in my life? What words or phrases resonate with me? What MIRACLE or part of the miracle do I feel connected to? Disconnected from?*):

_____

_____

_____

_____

_____

_____

_____

_____

_____

16.

Masterful

Individuals

Reappearing

Altered

Carrying

Loads of

Encouraging

Sentiments

Notes & Reflections (i.e. *how can I apply this in my life? What words or phrases resonate with me? What MIRACLE or part of the miracle do I feel connected to? Disconnected from?*):

_____

_____

_____

_____

_____

_____

_____

_____

_____

_____

17.

Metamorphosis of the
Interior
Realm
Amidst
Current
Lackadaisical
Emotion
Sordidness

Notes & Reflections (i.e. *how can I apply this in my life? What words or phrases resonate with me? What MIRACLE or part of the miracle do I feel connected to? Disconnected from?*):

_____

_____

_____

_____

_____

_____

_____

_____

18.
Maintaining
Inner
Reality
Although
Conditions of
Limitation
Exist
Seemingly

Notes & Reflections (i.e. *how can I apply this in my life? What words or phrases resonate with me? What MIRACLE or part of the miracle do I feel connected to? Disconnected from?*):

_____

_____

_____

_____

_____

_____

_____

_____

_____

19.
More
Internal
Reactions
Acting
Candidly
Lifting
Energy
Sweetly

Notes & Reflections (i.e. *how can I apply this in my life? What words or phrases resonate with me? What MIRACLE or part of the miracle do I feel connected to? Disconnected from?*):

_____

_____

_____

_____

_____

_____

_____

_____

_____

20.

Mellow

Innovative

Ravishing

Awesome

Courageous

Lavish

Excellent

Superb

Notes & Reflections (i.e. *how can I apply this in my life? What words or phrases resonate with me? What MIRACLE or part of the miracle do I feel connected to? Disconnected from?*):

_____

_____

_____

_____

_____

_____

_____

_____

_____

21.

Migraines

Irritability

Reactivity

Alarm

Calamity

Lunacy

Expelled and

Shushed

Notes & Reflections (i.e. *how can I apply this in my life? What words or phrases resonate with me? What MIRACLE or part of the miracle do I feel connected to? Disconnected from?*):

_____

_____

_____

_____

_____

_____

_____

_____

_____

22.

Monsters

Irrationally

Residing

Aimlessly

Catapulted and

Left

Empty of

Substance

Notes & Reflections (i.e. *how can I apply this in my life? What words or phrases resonate with me? What MIRACLE or part of the miracle do I feel connected to? Disconnected from?*):

_____

_____

_____

_____

_____

_____

_____

_____

23.
Meditative
Imaginative
Reflective
Allowing a
Considerable
Look and
Examination
Sight

Notes & Reflections (i.e. *how can I apply this in my life? What words or phrases resonate with me? What MIRACLE or part of the miracle do I feel connected to? Disconnected from?*):

_____

_____

_____

_____

_____

_____

_____

_____

_____

24.
Maturation of
Invisible
Roots in
Absence of
Cultivation and
Light
Emerging to the
Surface

Notes & Reflections (i.e. *how can I apply this in my life? What words or phrases resonate with me? What MIRACLE or part of the miracle do I feel connected to? Disconnected from?*):

_____

_____

_____

_____

_____

_____

_____

_____

_____

25.
Mystical
Insight
Reaffirming
Acknowledging
Continuous
Loyalty and
Enthusiasm for
Spirit

Notes & Reflections (i.e. *how can I apply this in my life? What words or phrases resonate with me? What MIRACLE or part of the miracle do I feel connected to? Disconnected from?*):

_____

_____

_____

_____

_____

_____

_____

_____

_____

26.

Mastermind
Interpretation
Resurging
Among
Creatures
Living in
Endless
Supply

Notes & Reflections (i.e. *how can I apply this in my life? What words or phrases resonate with me? What MIRACLE or part of the miracle do I feel connected to? Disconnected from?*):

_____

_____

_____

_____

_____

_____

_____

_____

_____

27.

Masterpiece
Iridescent
Renewing
Actualizing
Carefree
Lucid
Expressive
Stimulating

Notes & Reflections (i.e. *how can I apply this in my life? What words or phrases resonate with me? What MIRACLE or part of the miracle do I feel connected to? Disconnected from?*):

_____

_____

_____

_____

_____

_____

_____

_____

_____

28.
Movement
Intended to
Remove
Agitation
Completing
Life
Entirely
Scrupulously

Notes & Reflections (i.e. *how can I apply this in my life? What words or phrases resonate with me? What MIRACLE or part of the miracle do I feel connected to? Disconnected from?*):

_____

_____

_____

_____

_____

_____

_____

_____

29.
Maturing
Incremental
Righteousness
And
Clearly
Leaving
Enemies
Speechless

Notes & Reflections (i.e. *how can I apply this in my life? What words or phrases resonate with me? What MIRACLE or part of the miracle do I feel connected to? Disconnected from?*):

_____

_____

_____

_____

_____

_____

_____

_____

30.
Mending of
Illness and
Recovery of
Ailing
Corroding
Limbs
Eradicating
Sickness

Notes & Reflections (i.e. *how can I apply this in my life? What words or phrases resonate with me? What MIRACLE or part of the miracle do I feel connected to? Disconnected from?*):

_____

_____

_____

_____

_____

_____

_____

_____

_____

31.
Million-dollar
Idea
Resulting in
Accentuated
Cash flow
Little
Existence in
Squalor

Notes & Reflections (i.e. *how can I apply this in my life? What words or phrases resonate with me? What MIRACLE or part of the miracle do I feel connected to? Disconnected from?*):

_____

_____

_____

_____

_____

_____

_____

_____

32.
Markedly
Indulgent
Relaxed
Arranging
Calm
Laid-back
Effortless
Steps

Notes & Reflections (i.e. *how can I apply this in my life? What words or phrases resonate with me? What MIRACLE or part of the miracle do I feel connected to? Disconnected from?*):

_____

_____

_____

_____

_____

_____

_____

_____

_____

33.
Mindful
Interpretation of
Redundant &
Awkward
Complexities
Long
Established in
Summation

Notes & Reflections (i.e. *how can I apply this in my life? What words or phrases resonate with me? What MIRACLE or part of the miracle do I feel connected to? Disconnected from?*):

_____

_____

_____

_____

_____

_____

_____

_____

34.

Myopic

Intensive

Reasoning

Accelerating

Conviction

Logical

Esoteric

Setting

Notes & Reflections (i.e. *how can I apply this in my life? What words or phrases resonate with me? What MIRACLE or part of the miracle do I feel connected to? Disconnected from?*):

_____

_____

_____

_____

_____

_____

_____

_____

35.

Memorable
Illustrations
Reliving
Actively
Choosing to
Live
Eternally through
Self

74

Notes & Reflections (i.e. *how can I apply this in my life? What words or phrases resonate with me? What MIRACLE or part of the miracle do I feel connected to? Disconnected from?*):

_____

_____

_____

_____

_____

_____

_____

_____

_____

36.

Mystical

Inclination

Ready

Auspicious

Circulating

Luminously to

Encounter

Stupor

Notes & Reflections (i.e. *how can I apply this in my life? What words or phrases resonate with me? What MIRACLE or part of the miracle do I feel connected to? Disconnected from?*):

_____

_____

_____

_____

_____

_____

_____

_____

_____

Sometimes things that are inherent and are naturally occurring in nature can bring peace or clarity to our lives; including the situations we are in or the circumstances we are experiencing. Knowing that it takes a Bamboo tree five years to properly and firmly settle its roots into the ground before it shoots up ten feet tall and ten times stronger than most plants can ease our impatience when things aren't moving as quickly as we'd like, or when we aren't seeing the results we hoped for at the moment we wanted or felt we needed them.

As you read through the next few MIRACLES, take time to research the particular plant, animal, fruit, vegetable, tree, or phenomena. Find out what makes this being special. Appreciate its existence. Think about how its characteristics relate to you, your life, and your experience and begin to more fully understand and appreciate your existence as well.

37.

Moon

Icicles

River

Avalanche

Celestial

Lake

Earth

Sun

Notes & Reflections (i.e. *what do these beings represent in nature? How do they relate to me? Which phenomena resonate with me? What MIRACLE or part of the miracle do I feel connected to? Disconnected from? Why?*):

_____

_____

_____

_____

_____

_____

_____

_____

_____

38.

Maple

Ilex

Redwood

Acacia

Cedar

Lemongrass

Elm

Sycamore

Notes & Reflections (i.e. *what do these beings represent in nature? How do they relate to me? Which phenomena resonate with me? What MIRACLE or part of the miracle do I feel connected to? Disconnected from? Why?*):

_____

_____

_____

_____

_____

_____

_____

_____

39.

Moose

Iguana

Rabbit

Antelope

Camel

Lion

Elephant

Seal

Notes & Reflections (i.e. *what do these beings represent in nature? How do they relate to me? Which phenomena resonate with me? What MIRACLE or part of the miracle do I feel connected to? Disconnected from? Why?*):

_____

_____

_____

_____

_____

_____

_____

_____

_____

40.

Mango

Ice cream bean

Raspberry

Apricot

Cantaloupe

Lychee

Elderberry

Star fruit

Notes & Reflections (i.e. *what do these beings represent in nature? How do they relate to me? Which phenomena resonate with me? What MIRACLE or part of the miracle do I feel connected to? Disconnected from? Why?*):

_____

_____

_____

_____

_____

_____

_____

_____

_____

_____

41.

Mushroom
Iceberg lettuce
Rhubarb
Artichoke
Cassava
Leek
Eggplant
Squash

Notes & Reflections (i.e. *what do these beings represent in nature? How do they relate to me? Which phenomena resonate with me? What MIRACLE or part of the miracle do I feel connected to? Disconnected from? Why?*):

_____

_____

_____

_____

_____

_____

_____

_____

_____

42.

Mackerel

Indian Glassfish

Red Snapper

Alligator Gar

Catfish

Leaf Fish

Eel

Salmon

Notes & Reflections (i.e. *what do these beings represent in nature? How do they relate to me? Which phenomena resonate with me? What MIRACLE or part of the miracle do I feel connected to? Disconnected from? Why?*):

_____

_____

_____

_____

_____

_____

_____

_____

Give thanks Beautiful One, you are well into your journey. In these final ten weeks of M.I.R.A.C.L.E.S., allow yourself the freedom to truly express everything that you are seeing, hearing, and feeling as you travel through these pages and this part of your life. Reflect on your growth since you began this voyage. Notice the new aspects that you have attracted into your realm of being. Be conscious of those people, things, and circumstances that are no longer a part of your life. How do you feel? Pay attention and be in gratitude for that which is YOU.

43.

Marvelous

Intoxication of

Resilient

Abundance

Celebrating

Lively

Enjoyment &

Shouting

Notes & Reflections (i.e. *how can I apply this in my life? What words or phrases resonate with me? What MIRACLE or part of the miracle do I feel connected to? Disconnected from?*):

_____

_____

_____

_____

_____

_____

_____

_____

_____

44.
Muffled
Inside
Resting;
Arising, a
Chick
Leaving,
Exiting its
Shell

Notes & Reflections (i.e. *how can I apply this in my life? What words or phrases resonate with me? What MIRACLE or part of the miracle do I feel connected to? Disconnected from?*):

_____

_____

_____

_____

_____

_____

_____

_____

_____

45.

Making

It through

Rain

Atrocious

Climates

Lightening

Explosive

Storms

Notes & Reflections (i.e. *how can I apply this in my life? What words or phrases resonate with me? What MIRACLE or part of the miracle do I feel connected to? Disconnected from?*):

_____

_____

_____

_____

_____

_____

_____

_____

46.
Masquerading
In
Riveting
Alluring
Costumes; a
Local
Enraptured
Sign

Notes & Reflections (i.e. *how can I apply this in my life? What words or phrases resonate with me? What MIRACLE or part of the miracle do I feel connected to? Disconnected from?*):

_____

_____

_____

_____

_____

_____

_____

_____

_____

47.

Misguided

Interpretations

Righted by the

All-Mighty

Changing

Lenses so

Eyes can

See

Notes & Reflections (i.e. *how can I apply this in my life? What words or phrases resonate with me? What MIRACLE or part of the miracle do I feel connected to? Disconnected from?*):

_____

_____

_____

_____

_____

_____

_____

_____

48.
Morning
Inclinations
Rushing
Against
Countless
Latent
Escapades
Stored

Notes & Reflections (i.e. *how can I apply this in my life? What words or phrases resonate with me? What MIRACLE or part of the miracle do I feel connected to? Disconnected from?*):

_____

_____

_____

_____

_____

_____

_____

_____

_____

49.
Melting

Independent

Religions

Amid

Creation stories

Leaning towards

Embracing

Spirituality

Notes & Reflections (i.e. *how can I apply this in my life? What words or phrases resonate with me? What MIRACLE or part of the miracle do I feel connected to? Disconnected from?*):

_____

_____

_____

_____

_____

_____

_____

_____

50.

Magnanimous
Images
Reflecting
Arranged
Copying the
Likeness of your
Eternal
Soul

Notes & Reflections (i.e. *how can I apply this in my life? What words or phrases resonate with me? What MIRACLE or part of the miracle do I feel connected to? Disconnected from?*):

_____

_____

_____

_____

_____

_____

_____

_____

51.
Mindset
Incorporating the
Right now and
Ancient
Civilizations;
Longevity of our
Ever evolving
Source

Notes & Reflections (i.e. *how can I apply this in my life? What words or phrases resonate with me? What MIRACLE or part of the miracle do I feel connected to? Disconnected from?*):

_____

_____

_____

_____

_____

_____

_____

_____

_____

52.

Mission
Interpreted
Received
Accepted
Conspired
Legitimated
Effective
Surrendered

111

Time has elapsed since you first picked up this book and began practicing the art of remembering. You have undergone a metamorphosis and grown into a greater existence of your being. Is there more to do? Of course! The acquisition of knowledge for expansion and transformation is never complete. Along the way, you will encounter people, videos, books, quotes, and information that will allow for a deeper understanding of yourself, your world, and your Universe; the principles at work within it and how you can tap into the Universal Source for the unfoldment and expansion of your life while being a beneficial presence on the planet.

It is my desire that *Fifty-Two Weeks of M.I.R.A.C.L.E.S.* is one of those jewels on your journey.

Today's Date: _____

You are programmed for greatness. The blooming of a flower is both a miracle and a normal occurrence. So can be said for the hatching of a chick, the development of an embryo, the creation of a forest, and the sensational phenomenon of self revelation.

Fifty-Two Weeks of M.I.R.A.C.L.E.S. is about appreciating all that is wonderful and good on this planet. Through various spiritual outlets, we are able to more fully understand the Divine I AM and move closer to that which we come from. This book is designed to outline and highlight MIRACLES that exist and take place through, in, as and around you as phrases intended to be the weekly focus of contemplation, meditation, consideration, and reflection. Regardless of the activity you are immersed in; remember to remember that you are instrumental in a dynamic, unfolding world. To consciously draw from the Universal Source is to unlock and utilize the power of the infinite, which is already at your fingertips.